CU00780894

J.77 ARE YOU RECEIVING?

J.77 ARE YOU RECEIVING?

John Rowlinson

The Book Guild Ltd
Sussex, England

The Book Guild Ltd
25 High Street,
Lewes, Sussex

First published 1997
© John Rowlinson, 1997

Set in Palatino

Typesetting by Wordset
Hassocks, West Sussex

Printed in Great Britain by
Bookcraft (Bath) Ltd,
Avon

A catalogue record for this book is
available from the British Library

ISBN 1 85776 146 4

CONTENTS

1

Black Eye and Golf Clubs

The chief constable did not even look up from his desk and said, 'Why do you want to join the police?'

I mumbled in reply about public service and duty and that I wanted to do my bit, etc. He growled, 'You're in, if you pass the medical.'

It was rumoured that there was a constable serving in the force who had a conviction for assault on police. The story went that at his interview with the chief constable, he was asked, not unreasonably, if this was not a little unusual. He had explained that when he was in the army he was drinking alone in a pub when the locals had picked on him wearing his guards uniform. A fight had broken out and in the ensuing melee he had been obliged to defend himself and, sadly by mistake, of course he hit a police officer who had been sent to the scene.

The chief is then supposed to have said, 'Pride in the regiment is understandable, these things happen.'

In truth, the constable is supposed to have stood on the bar and offered to take on all present. It was said that it was pure coincidence that the chief officer had served with the Brigade of Guards.

The medical was a little more thorough than that of the forces and included the new colour-blindness test. The recruiting sergeant testing me told the doctor that I was colour-blind. The doctor looked at the test and asked the sergeant what number he could see. The reply resulted in the doctor telling him it was he who had a colour problem. I think it was then that I knew my police service was to be unusual and possibly even shorter than I first imagined.

*   *   *

Constable 697 duly reported to be issued with his uniform and was sent off to Sandgate to undertake his basic training. The same recruiting sergeant, showing no malice, pointed out to us recruits that each number issued to a constable had a history. The same numbers were issued again if there was a vacancy due to death, dismissal from the force or promotion. The last of these three was, in his view, impossible. Fate dictated that these numbers repeated themselves over the years, when the most recent wearer would suffer the same fate as his forebear. My number was associated with horses. It seems that one previous holder had stopped a runaway brewers dray at the bottom of Guildford High Street and another had stopped a runaway horse in Reigate. I was not very happy. I was, and still am, frightened of horses.

*   *   *

On my return from training I was posted to Weybridge. I don't think Weybridge or I were quite ready and one Saturday night I stood resplendent in my new shiny uniform directly under a streetlight outside a pub as the locals were being thrown out. One look at me was enough and in the space of only a few minutes any ill feelings there might have been with each other were soon lost on the 'common enemy', me. With torn uniform and a very large black eye, the young constable learnt always to keep out of the light, even more so at closing time.

In court the young officer walked up to the witness box to hardly concealed laughter as his black eye was now a nice red and blue. He gave his evidence and the accused were told that if they had anything to say to the officer this was their chance to say sorry and be fined a pound. They did not understand this, however, and when pressed by the magistrate for the second time, 'Are you sure there is nothing you would like to say to the officer?' they realized an answer was expected and their leader said, 'With a little bit of practice the lad will be quite good.' With this great compliment they were fined 50 pence.

*   *   *

Within a few weeks there was an incident that was to haunt me for the rest of my life. Every constable has to book his first motorist and I had to book a learner driver of a motor cycle, driving without L-plates. Pleased with myself for catching my first almost major criminal, I filled in the forms and served the summons on him at his home, where he lived with his Mum. A few days later he hanged himself. With the benefit of hindsight, and with life's experience in later years, I wish I had appreciated his situation and I hope that from that day onwards I had a much better approach to my fellow humans.

*   *   *

The river at Weybridge has been a major source of incident in police terms for years. My first experience was by the river bank one hot summer evening as a couple were enjoying themselves in a very intimate way in the long grass when a peeping Tom was seen climbing up a nearby tree to get a better view. I recall not being too sure what to do when a more experienced colleague arrived. Under his guidance we crept in the long grass to the foot of the tree. The couple were much to busy to take any notice. Our peeping Tom moved closer by sliding along the branch.

With that my fellow officer suddenly stood up and shouted, 'What are you doing? It was so loud that our Tom lost his grip and fell from the branch into the river near the bank. Having found out who he was, he was sent on his way soaking wet and we turned to the couple to see whether they wished to make a complaint. They, however, were at a very delicate part of the proceedings and had not heard or seen any of us, so we left them and I learnt that sometimes discretion saves paperwork.

*   *   *

Appearing in court can be quite an ordeal and to others it is no more than doing the shopping. There was a police motor cyclist who reported and prosecuted every motorist, cyclist and foot passenger who used the Queen's highway and was proud to take them to court and show off his zeal and devotion to duty, as he saw it. I saw him more than once reduce people to tears because they had touched the pavement with a tyre. He would point out at great length that standing on the pavement could have been a young child on his or her way home from school and by this most dangerous action he or she could have been maimed for life or worse, etc. He was, I always thought, the reason why police motor cyclists in those days were called 'black swine' even if you were being polite. This officer used to pride himself in having at least twelve or more offenders in court each Thursday. He was in his element if each case followed the other. He would step in and out of the witness box with a majestic air that only came from supreme confidence.

At the start of each case he would hold up the New

Testament as if he had just picked it up from Moses and say, 'I swear by Almighty God that the evidence I shall give . . .' He would then pick up his pocketbook and give his evidence.

One day he picked up his pocketbook instead of the testament and started, 'I swear by . . .,' when the clerk to the court told him to stop and pointed out to him that he was sure that the Almighty would possibly understand that his notebook was almost as good as the testament, but the law of the United Kingdom was quite clear that the oath should be taken with the testament.

* * *

I had moved to Weybridge with a number of other young men and we all lived in single accommodation at the back of the police station. At first it was thought kind of the authorities to give us a roof over our heads and food twice a day. However, if there was ever any need for additional police in times of strife it will come as no surprise as to where these additional men were found.

There was one man whom I think caused me more trouble than any other man before or since. He was small, had been in the special air service, was a state registered nurse and was so fit that when there was an incident when he was giving chase to some young absconders late one night – he, in full uniform, coat, boots etc., they in shorts, and running shoes, after a mile they dived into the Thames and he followed. Up the other side and over the fields he was still following until after about three miles they collapsed and he slightly out breath, told them he 'hadn't enjoyed himself so much for days'.

He did have a number of unusual hobbies. One was taxidermy and another practical jokes and he took great delight in sharing his exhibits with others. These included giant spiders that he had caught whilst in Malaya, together with snakes, all suitably preserved, and after night duty you would find them in your bed or suitably coiled up or hanging down from the lampshade. I recall him being in some trouble for being seen with his uniform jacket off, whilst on duty, skinning a badger that had been killed in a road traffic accident. I was also in trouble for telling him about the accident in the first place.

He was also a very good impersonator of birds and if on night duty heard an owl hooting, he replied. The owl called him and three days later the local paper reported that Weybridge still had a rural life as only the other night the local expert had been entranced by two owls courting each other nearby.

*   *   *

The golf club at St George's Hill was reached by a steep road, each side of which was dense undergrowth. The clubhouse had been broken into a number of times and all of us on night duty were told to pay specific attention to it and two of us were to meet there at 3 a.m. Upon my arrival I saw a policeman standing on a golf trolley. He was holding the handle whilst his two legs were astride the wheels. He was confident that if I gave him a little push he would gather speed and coast to the bottom of the hill. It seemed a reasonable idea at the time, so with a little push he was off down the hill, swerving from side to side. Then he lost control and crashed through the undergrowth with enough noise to awaken the whole of Weybridge, let alone the dead. The lights came on in the clubhouse and a voice called down to me, 'Don't worry I have called the police.'

In due course the sergeant, inspector and others arrived. I recall saying something along the lines that we heard a noise and my companion had gone to investigate. There had been a lot of noise as if he was after someone. A few moments later he appeared, uniform torn, face scratched and murmured that he had tried but had lost him in the bushes. The inspector congratulated him for having a go and gave me a look to indicate that I had let the side down.

*   *   *

People go away on holiday and at that time it seemed that a large number told the police and it was one's duty to visit as many vacant houses as possible during a tour of duty. It could be quite interesting walking around other people's property and I recall walking round one when I heard the bath water running away. Knocking on the door at last produced a face at the upstairs bathroom window and I was told by a young man that he was the son of the family down from Oxford. They were in Cornwall and he would be joining them tomorrow. Happy, I continued on my way and met the duty sergeant. I duly told him my story to demonstrate my skills in interviewing, only to be told that we had better get back there as the family had no son and always went to Bognor for their holidays. A young man was arrested just before he left the house with his booty.

*   *   *

The large houses were always more fun to visit and I recall walking around the back of one owned by General Sir Somebody and saw a squirrel sitting on the lawn. I thought that if I stood still and slowly drew my truncheon I could give it quite a surprise. As I had my arm behind my head a voice boomed behind me, 'Hunting officer.'

*   *   *

There are some people who are frightened by the dark. Most of us get used to it but it would be unusual for a police officer to suffer from it. I recall, however being asked to stay in the garden of an empty house after dusk to watch, and note what happened. At the time I was not too pleased and after about three-quarters of an hour I heard a noise approaching and there was a policeman on his cycle, riding up the drive and round the side, singing at the top of his voice, holding a torch in one hand, switched on, another on a clip on his uniform jacket. The cycle had a battery lamp and at least two other lamps, all switched on. He looked like something between Father Christmas and a mobile light disco. He got round the house without stopping, at an impressive speed, and went down the drive with a row of red lights shining brightly. When I met the sergeant shortly afterwards I recall him not batting an eyelid and told me we would keep it between ourselves, wouldn't we? A constable resigned shortly afterwards.

*   *   *

It is important to recall that in those times much was achieved by nice straightforward blackmail or threat, just hinted at, not real of course. A young constable wanted to grow a beard and duly submitted a written request to grow a full set. The regulations at the time required a sailor's type beard as depicted on the Player's cigarette packet. The trouble was that you had to leave duty clean-shaven and return to duty with the full set. An appearance in between was classed as 'stubble' and the offender was reported for not being fit for duty, by appearance. Our young constable had thought of this and intended to go on holiday for two weeks and he hoped on his return, with his beard fast growing, that there would be no problem. Much to his surprise his request was met by the superintendent of the division requesting him to call on him at his home. It was almost unheard of for such a meeting to be requested – ordered maybe, but why at this home? The young constable duly appeared and accepted a cup of tea from Mrs Superintendent and was then directed to the greenhouse. He was met with a genuine friendly gardener, not the man he had been warned about. He was told that his request would be granted. Where was he going on holiday? The conversation got round to his police life, his hopes for the future and his record so far and then he was asked, almost in passing, how many senior officers did he know who had a full set. Between them they could recall no senior officers, one inspector, one sergeant, both long in service and ex-navy, otherwise there really did seem to be very few men who had made it. But never mind, he felt that if anyone could do it the young constable stood as good a chance as any. He left the house, had a good holiday and history suggests that he never did in fact grow that set.

*   *   *

One afternoon I was informed that I was going to be posted to Leatherhead. I recall wondering whether this entailed brown paper and a stamp and asked if there was any reason for this and was told that a young officer had just left the force in a hurry. He was going to Leatherhead so *you* take his place. A single man was allowed one half day to move to a new station. A married man one whole day! It seems that a single man should have been able to put all his possessions on a barrow and wheel them to his new digs. That's how the story goes and I do know that before I joined you had to put in writing for permission to marry. The young lady was interviewed to make sure that she would be suitable as a constable's wife and a bank book had to be produced – I think with the sum of £100 therein.

Times had changed, although I recall that when my time came I had to inform my employers of my intended, including date and place of birth, so they could check.

*   *   *

I found living in digs very different and working in a small station where the compliment was some 20 men in total. On my first night duty I was advised by a colleague who only had a few months to go before retirement that I should put my supper on a shelf. His enquiry as to its make-up should have aroused my suspicion. At 3 a.m., however, I returned only to find the whole lot consumed and a very surprised station duty man told me he had eaten them by mistake and that by the way, my choice for refreshment was not very good. He was one of the most work-shy men I had met. He would not investigate a stolen pedal cycle in case he found the offender and had to go to court to give evidence as he was about to retire in spite of it being pointed out to him that he had still over twelve months to go.

*   *   *

I put in a written request to be considered for motor cycle duty. The reply has always puzzled me a little. It said, 'Prove yourself a policeman.' Perhaps I should have gone to the doctor but presumed that I had to prove that I was good at my job first. Within a few weeks I had my chance. I was third reserve for motor cycle duty, from 6 p.m. to 2 a.m. and around 1 a.m. there was a suspicious car parked near Headley Heath. Upon my approach a very familiar moustache appeared at the window not unlike my inspector's, and a voice said, 'Not that bloody keen.' I remember not recording that vehicle check and have

10

wondered from time to time whether there was any connection with this incident and my transfer to full-time motor cycle duties shortly afterwards and decided coincidence is quite remarkable.

At least J.77 was mine for eight hours a day!

2

Condom and Nudes

Headley Heath has a number of memories for me, including one December morning when sitting on the police bike I saw a couple in my rear-view mirror emerge from the heath carrying two or three bunches of holly. Upon seeing me they unzipped their jackets and put the holly inside and I could see that this caused a little pain. I decided to sit it out and in a few minutes they walked over to their motor cycle, looking at me all the time. I felt that they were rather keen for me to move off. A few more moments, and again in great pain, he kick-started the bike and with further grimaces they snuggled behind each other and moved off. I followed and drew alongside them and asked the rider if he liked masochism. He gave me a very unusual look as I drove off and you can see that, very slowly, I was becoming a good police officer! I still do not believe that a prosecution would have been the right answer but a more usual caution might have met the situation in a more legal sense.

*   *   *

From time to time car duty was undertaken and it will be understood that there were many calls over the radio to incidents and upon arrival there is no sign of the incident.

Early one morning we received a radio call that a large brown bear was in the middle of the road in a village just outside Dorking and upon arrival you can imagine my dismay when I saw, sitting in the middle of the road on this sunny morning, the largest brown bear that I had ever seen. There were members of the public watching and they expect their police to do something. So, with some reluctance, I got out of the car, asking myself whether to call for the army or a zoo, when a little girl appeared and ran straight up to the bear. I almost stopped breathing. She got it by the ear and said, 'Bruno, you naughty boy,' and led him away. She must have been all of eight years of age. There are times when one feels incapable of dealing with a situation, in spite of training.

*   *   *

A radio call from the railway station, 'Disturbance', revealed a train stopped, all the doors open and the passengers gathered around one carriage where a young lady, with a slightly torn top, was screaming and crying that a man sitting inside the train compartment had assaulted her.

'He's still there,' she shouted.

Inside was a rather portly, elderly man and as I got inside the carriage he said in a very calm voice, 'Officer, before you say anything, please look and note the ash on my cigar.' The ash was some two inches long and the railway staff confirmed that he had asked the same of them.

In due course it appeared that our complainant had tried similar acts before and when confronted she confirmed that most men paid up, 'Five pounds or so, to shut me up!'

I remember asking her if she had had her bluff called before. 'Once,' she said. 'He said, "OK, it's worth it", and she had fled.

*   *   *

In my early days at Leatherhead, whilst on the beat, most weekends each evening an elderly couple used to sit on a bench watching the traffic go by. I used to talk to them and it seemed that they just wanted something to do.

One summer evening the elderly lady ran up the street about midnight wearing her nightie and shouting out, 'They are all listening to us.' I managed to calm her down and went back home with her only to be told that her house was 'full of them'. I shouted out that it was the police and told her that they had gone. She agreed and went happily indoors and from that day on we waved to each other.

Almost a year later I went on duty around 6.45 a.m. and the duty sergeant, much to the amusement of my colleagues, informed me that my 'girlfriend' was waiting in reception and had been there for over an hour and would speak only to me. I sat down beside her and she told me she had been naughty. I explained that we all are from to time. She talked about being really naughty and I asked her what she had done. After a lot of coaxing she explained that she had got cross with her husband and had hit him on the head with an axe and she thought she had split him in half. I can still see the faces of certain police officers when we rushed to her house and found that she was right. The scene in the bedroom would not be believed if shown on a modern horror film. Her husband was just alive but died a few days later. She went to Broadmoor.

*   *   *

Around 2 p.m. one sunny weekend afternoon I was sent to the A246 where there had been a report of a naked lady sitting by the road. I recall several cars asking if I needed assistance. Upon driving up to some traffic lights, there, on the nearside of the road, was a young lady, naked, sitting on a canvas chair, knitting. I was rather surprised and nearly went across a red traffic light, falling off the police bike at the same time.

As I walked up to her she gave me a nice smile as I explained, not very clearly, that there had been a complaint about her lack of clothes and she was felt to be a little of a distraction to passing motorists. She apologized and asked me to pass her top and shorts to her. This I did and at the same time saw the duty sergeant appear to see if I needed any help. We then saw, lying on the grass verge, a young man also unclothed, fast asleep. We woke him up and as the young lady was packing the car the sergeant took the young man on one side and asked if he was all right, as not many men could fall fast asleep beside an unclothed young lady on a sunny day in the country even if they were a little close to a main road.

I recall that the incident was written up: 'Young couple given advice, no further action necessary'.

*   *   *

I was still awaiting my prophesied encounter with a horse. As the months passed I almost had forgotten about it. One lunchtime that metallic voice on the speaker made my heart pound.

'High Street, horse thrown rider, animal berserk'.

Upon arrival, the rider was lying on the ground injured but able to talk. An ambulance had been called. Meanwhile the horse was rearing and bucking and with the help of passers-by and me, we tethered the poor animal to a traffic light. Its flanks were spouting blood, with great slithers of glass sticking out where, in its panic it had backed into the plate glass window of a shop, which of course, had broken and the pile of plate glass all over the pavement plus the gathering of watchers just added to the general confusion. I managed to get a message out for a vet, assistance arrived and one of my colleagues, much to my relief, had an affinity with horses.

The vet arrived. The rider was suffering from shock. The horse was led away and all recovered. I still find it difficult to understand however, why an ex-racehorse that was highly strung anyway should for the first lesson of getting used to traffic be ridden back and forth through a busy high street and, on the second journey, have taken fright. I'm surprised it managed the first. The rider saw nothing unusual in this and felt it was a perfectly safe training exercise to undertake where the public and traffic would provide the real-life situation.

Around 11 p.m. one summer evening, coming past a local beauty spot, a car pulled out in front of J.77 and, as it gathered speed, out of the driver's window came with a great 'plop', a used condom that caught on the windscreen of the motor cycle and then hung down like a Christmas decoration.

My reaction was not too surprising and the car was pulled over and stopped. I pointed out to the driver that a very unfortunate accident had happened and what was he going to do about it? At this his lady passenger slowly slipped from sight under the dashboard. The driver quickly got out of his car and walked with all speed up to the police bike and untangled the decoration hanging from the windscreen. I pointed out that the screen needed a wipe and his handkerchief did the job well. He was still holding the condom. I felt that he was feeling rather embarrassed at this point he went to throw the item onto the ground. I pointed out to him that if he did, he would be reported for throwing litter, among other things. He then produced a matchbox, opened it, and slowly coiled the condom into the box and then closed it.

Together we returned to his car to examine his driving licence. His companion looked very uncomfortable crouched under the windscreen but never said a word. The driver asked me if anything was going to happen. I replied that I felt enough had happened already and I only hoped that when he got home his wife did not ask him for a light. He thanked me, I cannot really think why.

*   *   *

A story I am always reluctant to relate concerns a very bad winter's day and night and how early one morning, driving a car, we were advised that we would be picking up a member of Parliament, a Cabinet Minister, and taking him to the outskirts of London when he would continue his car journey with the Metropolitan Police. Picture if you will in the early hours of the morning a police car with all its doors open, while two police officers cleaned out crisps and cigarette packets, sweet wrappers etc., and did their best to get the interior of the car in a reasonable state. We duly picked up our VIP passenger and our journey continued in complete silence for some miles.

I was driving and looking at my colleague out of the corner of my eye as we passed the countryside covered in deep snow and there, in a field in front of us, were some cows and I said out loud. 'Those poor moo cows, just look at them!'

I realized what I had said. My colleague was trying not to laugh, our passenger grunted and buried his nose further into the papers he was reading. I had, of course, thought, for a moment that my young children were in the car with me.

We arrived on time, met our Metropolitan car, and there were commanders, superintendents all there to see that our guest got to his important meeting and one of them asked him if he had a good journey and he said, 'You know, I think the officers in Surrey, get younger and younger.'

I was pleased that the questioner did not understand the reply.

*   *   *

One night duty at around 3 a.m. a 'smash and grab' took place in the high street and the culprit was seen running down the street with watches and jewellery falling to the ground as he fled. The police dog arrived; the cream of the force, he had won almost all championships over the year.

The dog tracked the thief by sniffing the watches, etc. I remember we reminded the handler that we had managed to do that. Near the river, by some houses with a small wooden fence separating the front garden from the road the dog stopped. We all waited in expectation and the dog promptly relieved itself against the fence, where upon our thief, I'm almost sure trying not to laugh, gave himself up. The dog's reputation throughout the force was greatly enhanced when it was known that its tinkle caught criminals!

*   *   *

There was a rather unusual sequel to this when, with perhaps understandable malice a few days later I emerged from a meal break at the police station that had taken no more than three-quarters of an hour before reporting by radio that duty was being resumed, only to find that a large police dog was guarding J.77 and that there was no way that I was allowed to get near enough to it to use the radio. The dog snarled and refused all types of bribe, from biscuits to chocolate, to move. After some fifteen minutes I gave up and went to report a fault with my radio, when up came the handler, took charge of his dog, and I got a rocket for an unauthorized extended meal break and the entire force area heard me being asked if the wine had been chilled for my banquet.

*　　*　　*

I will only admit to one case of rather enjoying booking a motorist for speeding. I had asked him his name and he replied, 'Tortize.' I asked to see his licence and his name was 'Tortoise'. I did give a little smile when the local paper carried the story: 'Tortoise, caught speeding on main A 24 road'.

Early one morning I was called to a domestic dispute where a lorry driver had been asked to reverse his lorry over a rose bed, across an immaculate lawn and drop the complete lorry load of sand into the living-room of a large bungalow via the double doors facing the patio.

The owner explained that he was holding a party the theme of which was the desert, having taken up the carpet, he wanted the sand spread evenly over the wood block floor, up to the power sockets. The driver of the lorry, with some concern, was reluctant to comply without a little evidence available from an independent person. I carried out all the checks that I could, from who owned the house, etc. I also was concerned that I might aid and abet a good practical joke. All was well and I hope the party went well.

*　　*　　*

Every town has its characters and I recall one who was involved in many adventures, some running very close to breaking the law and others well over the edge. There was nothing that he would not turn his hand to and I recall he borrowed a van and collected some 12 piglets from a farm and forgot to pay for them, which could be due to his time of collection being around 11.30 p.m. The owner, a little concerned, telephoned the police and, sure enough, just in front of me was the van concerned. I pulled up alongside and signalled for the driver to stop. This he ignored and accelerated a little to some 25 m.p.h. I think the police car was in second gear when we came to a rather sharp bend and, as the van heeled over the back doors opened and out tumbled piglets. It seemed as if there were hundreds. We braked hard and so did the van. We jumped out and got hold of the driver and asked what he was doing with piglets.

He looked up and down the road, where they were all running around and making an incredible noise, and answered, 'What piglets?'

The second incident concerned a safe at a factory and he and his gang broke into the premises in the early hours, tried to open the safe, and having no luck, decided to load it on to the van and drive it away to a secluded spot where they could open it without interruption. Unfortunately, upon trying to load it onto the van, they dropped it upon the foot of one of their members who cried out in real agony and started to hop around, holding the damaged foot, screaming his head off. The noise was such that the entire estate woke up, the police were called and, upon arrival, everyone concerned was shouting at the injured man to 'shut up'.

I have always envied those with a quick mind, those who can get out of trouble with a ready answer.

It was trouble if you were caught talking, especially if the talking was verging on gossiping, and to be caught talking to a young lady was almost instant death, yet a colleague was caught 'chatting up' a young lady, and when confronted by a very irate sergeant he calmly explained that he was just answering her enquiry as to how she could join the police force.

Loneliness has always been a sad fact of life and, especially, when the years start to tell. There was a lady who used to come into the police station to report the loss of her pension book each Tuesday. When she left, the book was always found by the counter where she had been standing. Each week, the book was returned to her at home, when you found that you were the only person she could feel at ease talking to, often for days on end.

There was another lady who always drove her car into town each week and on the way home would stop by a field and talk to the horses. She would then walk home and report that the car had been stolen. We would recover it, return to her and be congratulated on our efficiency.

*   *   *

Work can cause problems at home and if there was ever a case of talking, perhaps the following helps to demonstrate the need. I had not stopped the kitchen tap from dripping before going on duty one afternoon and, like all taps the drip, drip became very annoying. Just before the end of duty I had been sent to an office premises where a lift engineer had been working most of the evening trying to get the lifts operational for the next day. Due to a tragic set of circumstances, he had severed both his hands from the wrists as the lift had suddenly come down on him whilst he was working. He was alive and undergoing an operation when I had to visit his young wife and their three young children and break the news to them. Having done everything I could to assist, I returned home to be greeted with 'That tap, is driving me mad!' The words that followed can easily be guessed. The moral must be 'get your word in first'.

*　　*　　*

Around 5 p.m. one sunny summer afternoon I was called to visit a local householder who was sure that a light aircraft had engine trouble and was going to make a forced landing. Upon arrival, I was not really sure what had been seen or heard and asked the informant, I hope not in a sarcastic manner, if he would know if an aircraft were in distress.

He replied, 'I think so. My name is Barnes Wallis.'

He was right. A light aircraft had made a forced landing nearby.

3

Donkeys and Teddies

Paperwork has and always be a problem and one afternoon I was called to an accident involving a van and a donkey. Upon arrival, a young girl who had been injured was taken to hospital. The van was parked on the pavement behind the donkey, who was unconcerned and eating the grass on the verge. On talking to the driver of the van, I did wonder if I should tie the donkey to something and started to walk towards it, whereupon it lashed out with its hind legs and kicked the radiator of the van back onto the engine and, if that was not enough, it lashed out again and broke both headlights. The driver was most upset and blamed me. I remember I put the donkey down in the accident report as vehicle 2, and wrote 'vehicle 2 kicked out with hind legs and hit vehicle I, etc.'

I had at least three calls from headquarters and the Home Office to say that my accident would not fit into any of their statistics and was I sure of the facts? It seems that it was appreciated that animals could be injured but not that they could cause injury to motor vehicles.

*   *   *

Accidents are always a problem but even more so if the vehicle concerned is a police one and no other vehicle is involved. There was a force instruction that when two officers in a car that needed to reverse, the passenger should get out and make sure that the vehicle could reverse in safety without mishap. It is not difficult to imagine that on nights, cold dark evenings, every officer was keen to get out of the vehicle every time you went round the back of business premises. The instruction was almost always ignored but, nevertheless, there it was in writing. One Saturday around 3 p.m. I swept my police car around the back of a factory and reversed in style straight into a concrete pillar. They seem to be made just short enough not be seen when sitting in the driving seat. A large dent was there in the middle of the rear bumper, for all to see. Every garage that might of be of use was unable to help due to the day and time. The trouble was that both of us would be in trouble and we would be obliged to report the accident at the end of duty, at the very latest 11 p.m. At meal break time I remember reversing the car tight up to a wall at a police station so that the damage could not be seen. Up to 10.30 p.m. we rehearsed our stories, and at 10.35 we were sent to an accident on the Dorking by-pass. Upon arrival vehicles were all over the road but there were no injuries. I parked the police car on the centre reservation with blue light flashing. Within a few moments there was a loud crash and a young man had driven his car straight up the back of the police car. He had been watching the scene! He even remarked during the detail of a report that he thought I was 'jolly good' not to be upset about the damage to the Police car. Little did he know.

There was a rather interesting postscript to this incident in that we had to give our views on the best safety position to be used when parking police vehicles at night when dealing with accidents!

*   *   *

When people talk of modern technology I remember one night duty at headquarters upon a short visit. I was ushered into a special room full of teleprinters that were in contact with most police forces throughout the world.

I was allowed to choose one and Belgium was chosen and my guide typed out a message of greeting from the Surrey Constabulary to the chief gendarme of Liege, timed at 3 a.m. and, indeed, within only a few moments a teleprinter started to chatter and my guide ripped off the sheet and there was written, 'Why don't you piss off? Look at the time!'

* * *

Accidents seem to cause distress to everyone and not only to those involved. Much has been written on the subject and I do not feel able to offer any real advice but think one or two incidents might give a different picture.

The first involves a young lady who, when riding a scooter, ran into the back of a parked lorry and caused herself major injury including a great loss of blood from a leg injury. Coming upon the scene shortly after it had happened, I had to put pressure on the artery on her thigh. She went to hospital, recovered and that was the end of the matter. Some months later I was invited to a party by a girlfriend. There was this young lady who promptly told everyone that I had greatly enjoyed giving her first aid and asked how many other incidents had I dealt with. I recall leaving as soon as possible, rather red faced, and trying to explain. Any reputation I may have had was now in tatters.

It is hard to describe that cold feeling inside when dealing with major injury in accidents: the lady blinded by the windscreen glass in her face, holding your hand while she was cut out of the car, the trouble being that she had broken glass in her hand which she pressed into your hand as she tried to cope with her distress, and all you wanted to do was to shout out with your own pain and snatch your hand away.

That feeling of hopelessness when you were unable to get people out of a car on fire; the rage you felt when at the scene of a fatal accident, within minutes of the bodies being removed, motorists passing the scene at speeds that were unbelievable, often with all occupants gazing out of the windows with serious curiosity. It took some time for me to realize that you did the same when you became a member of the public.

Then there is the car that careers off the road across the verge and pavement and into the river – one dead, several just living, car some two hours later pulled out the river, due to a steep bank, only to find a dog on a lead trapped on the front radiator grill, dead of course. The realization that if there is a lead where is the person taking it for a walk? Colleagues return to help look and the final discovery of the owner some two hundred yards down stream also dead. These incidents did make me wonder whether if your time is up there is little that can be done.

At this time there were mods and rockers riding about on motor cycles and scooters, giving and receiving their share of trouble – very similar with every generation that comes along. In this case a car had overturned with occupants trapped. A motley crew on motor cycles arrived in black leather jackets, some 50 in all. 'Can we help?' I have never seen so much effort given with humour and strength to right the car, doing everything I asked. When it was finished there was the roar of bikes and the usual comment at that time, 'See you in court, mate!'

*   *   *

The powers that be had started to consider me to be sent

away on courses. I was not sure whether it was just to get me out of the way or they just needed someone to send. I believe the latter was more the case and on a course for instructors, as part of the final test, it was necessary to give a lecture for ten minutes and end on time by introducing the next speaker. As I droned on I saw that the time was just right to introduce the next speaker and at that very moment I forgot his name. As panic started to set in I remembered that the name had a connection with a window. By this time I had to give a name and said, 'Sergeant Window' whereupon my fellow officers squeaked with mirth and as I sat down the next speaker rose to give his talk. His name was Sergeant Curtain. I believe for the rest of my service he felt that I had done it on purpose and I was not forgiven.

There was a training film at the centre and in one shot there was a scene of the lord lieutenant getting out of a carriage when his sword came between his legs and he nearly fell over. We found out that if you played the film backwards the resulting pictures were a real threat to the silent movies. One day, showing the film backwards for the umpteenth time, the door opened and there was the chief constable with the lord lieutenant being taken round the training centre. They all laughed at the good joke but have you ever felt that your cards were marked thereafter?

One afternoon when reporting for duty at 3.00 p.m. I was told that I was to remain on patrol on the A24 between two roundabouts that were only some two miles apart. No reason was given and all afternoon the patrol continued up and down the road. Several incidents happened nearby but each time my plea to do something was refused. At 6.00 p.m. I was allowed a meal break but afterwards the patrol had to be continued. At around 9.00 p.m. I came across a patrol car whose crew were also very frustrated in being confined to the area. Several incidents happened each time both of us were not required.

At 10.00 p.m. we both received a call to go to a large private house on an estate nearby and contact the informant, the chief constable.

Upon arrival, within four minutes we were greeted by the chief and several other guests all wearing evening dress. We saluted him and he turned to the others and said, 'There you are. We aim to respond to any call within seven minutes.'

Again, coincidence did seem to crop up every now and again. There were of course many incidents of drunken driving, all very sad for everyone but two come to mind as being different. The first concerned a motorist who jumped a traffic light and crashed through a shop window, the car ending up at the rear of the shop. Upon my arrival our motorist was sitting amongst the toys and with his arm round a very large teddy bear who, he explained, had been his friend since childhood. They had been through thick and thin together over the years and where one went so did the other. Teddy was arrested alongside his companion and both taken to the police station. In due course the teddy watched from sitting on the charge room table as his mate being charged and then led away to the cells. Within a few hours our motorist was shouting that he was the friend of everyone in authority and we all would be unemployed very soon as he was not without influence.

At 10.00 a.m. the next morning he appeared in court having told the court he was not guilty and a bigger miscarriage of justice was difficult to imagine. The police inspector whispered to the usher who disappeared for a few moments and returned carrying a very large teddy bear which he placed on the seat beside me. Our motorist took one look at my companion and changed his plea to guilty. At least it saved the rate payers a few pounds.

The second incident is hard to believe but took place one afternoon just after the breath test came into being and both my colleague and I had learnt the new caution and were well-versed as to the provisions which required an arrested driver to be taken without delay to the nearest police station for further tests.

We then encountered a motorist going the wrong side of a keep left sign. The breath test proved positive so in the police car he went and at the moment a smash and grab raid took place and almost at once the car involved crossed our path going at great speed, we gave chase and advised HQ and as the chase developed our friend got very excited and shouted, 'Look out, he's turning left, no right, etc.' Other cars joined in the chase and some ten miles on the car ran off the road through a hedge. As we screeched to a halt, he was first out and ran up to the passenger door and arrested the occupant. We, with other assistance, arrested the remainder. On the return journey we realized that what had taken place hardly met the provisions of the breath test, so back at the scene of the keep left sign we decided to give our passenger, who was very pleased with his arrest, and kept on telling us he had not had so much fun in years, another breath test. We could then let him drive home. He failed this test as well so we were left with me driving his car to his home when he could not tell his wife enough of his car chase etc. We asked her not to let him drive and drove away with great shouts and waving of arms from our motorist.

Well, you can't win them all and I did wonder how many friends and relations had to listen to his story and whether they believed him.

*   *   *

There are many incidents that take place which are very trivial but from time to time come back to the mind. One concerns stopping a speeding motorist and duly completing the booking and off he drove, in a mood. As I walked back to J.77 not feeling very happy, in spite of popular belief that on such occasions a great thrill is felt, I realized I had left my motor cycle gloves on the roof of the car as I had written down all the details. There was little else to do but follow the car until they fell off the roof, I was not prepared to stop him again and ask him, 'Can I have my gloves back, please?' I tried of course to follow at a discreet distance but he of course saw me and as a result was not going to get caught again, so travelled well within the speed limits, resulting of course with the gloves refusing to move off the roof. I followed for over three miles and was well into the metropolitan police area, thinking what am I going to say if I am called to an incident back into the force area. Then, as I was really thinking of having to give up, he swept round a roundabout and off the roof came the gloves and passing motorists must have enjoyed the sight of a 'black swine' rummaging on the grass verge, pretending that he was looking for some vital clue for a major crime that was bound to be front page news tomorrow.

4

Pornography and Treacle

Officers, whether in the army or the police force, came in many sizes and either earned or had no respect from their men. There was one inspector I would describe in today's words as a 'Hooray Henry' and did not have the respect that he would have liked. He was fair but seemed too speak with a very much upper crust accent which put you thinking of him as just acceptable. There were a lot worse.

One day I was called with others to a plane crash, and upon arrival in the middle of mud, woodland and high trees there was this unforgettable scene, which is difficult to describe, I suspect mainly because the mind does not want to return to the nightmare of devastation, fire, smoke, plane debris, personal luggage and effects, dolls, trousers, teddybears smouldering, burning suitcases and bodies lying not only on the ground but suspended in the trees, legless and armless corpses, some smouldering, others with no signs of injury.

I was allocated with another to remove the body of a young lady which had been impaled upon a tree some twenty feet high. With axes we took it in turn to chop down the tree about four feet above the corpse which was also smouldering. With each strike of the axe a little more of the insides of the lady spilled out upon the ground.

Several senior officers passed by and remarked that we

had got a good one and hurried on by. Then our Hooray Henry Inspector arrived and took one look at us, took off his hat and jacket, took each of our axes in turn and helped cut down the tree. We were able to get just a little respite and from that day onwards no man had gained my respect more than he and I learnt why so many men were prepared to follow their officers from the trenches in the First World War. It was hard to find any humour in that incident and I could still describe every detail of the corpse in airline uniform looking down on us from the trees, with that skeleton grin made worse in the darkness by the flickering fires and long shadows.

*　　*　　*

When riding J.77 if you were bored, you could always catch up to the car in front when the children were looking out of the rear window. When you had settled down a nice distance behind you would stick out your tongue, just a little. A slow grin would appear on their faces, they would turn round and say something to the driver and almost at once the rear brake lights would come one. One had to brake just as the children turned their heads, otherwise the accident report would be difficult to complete and any career you may have had could well come to an early end.

I found delivering a 'death message' one of the more unpleasant duties and if the need arose at the start of a tour of duty my morale was fairly low for the rest of the day. When training, much of the information about how to cope with a situation was tinged with a little black humour, and the 'death message' was no exception. You did not knock on the door and enquire whether widow Brown lived there? When the lady replied, 'No' you did not say, 'Well you are now.' In this way anything you did must be better and if possible if was often a good idea to knock on a neighbour's door and find out if they were on friendly terms. If so, ask the neighbour to come with you as you had some very sad news to give. It is very much to the credit of people that I do not recall ever having been refused, if they could help.

There were however a number of instances when the guidelines did not help. I was asked to deliver such a 'death message' to an address, when it seemed that the man in the household had been killed in a road traffic accident, papers in his coat gave the address, the driving licence however gave another. I called at the neighbour, however. The people next door had only been there for two days. There was a husband, wife and two children. I knocked on the door and a little girl of four explained to me through the letter box, as she was not allowed to open the door to strangers, that Daddy had gone in the car to get them fish and chips for supper. I slowly managed to get her to tell me that she was alone with her little brother and at lunchtime they had all gone to an airport to see mummy off on an aeroplane.

With the help of female colleagues, and having broken into the house having explained through the letter box what we were going to do, and we knew daddy would not be cross, we took the children to a colleague's home where we knew his wife would help us – no duty social services in those days. We searched the house for any address or telephone number, and all the signs seemed to confirm that the family had only just moved in.

Getting somewhat desperate, I decided to open the post and there was a 'welcome to your new home card' with a name and, luckily, an address. a call to directory enquiries gave us a number and a call confirmed a relation but they knew only that the airport was Heathrow and the flight was most likely to be to Sweden where they knew the wife was going to visit a long-standing friend. Heathrow confirmed flight and the plane was just about to arrive. The poor wife was told of the accident and that we were looking after her children for her. In due course she was able to give us the address of the grandparents. Again, another difficult telephone call and the children were collected.

One afternoon I went to deliver a message to a lady telling her that her male friend had died, following an accident. She lived in a flat and, again, none of the neighbours who were in was able to help. I felt well, at least it is not a relation, knocked on the door and a young lady appeared and as in a lot of cases the uniform carries a message of its own. She looked at me, screamed and rushed towards the open window and started to fumble with the curtains. I seemed to take for ever to catch on but did, and got her to sit down. The story slowly unfolded that she had told her boyfriend that all was over between them, had left him in Portsmouth and had come home. About an hour earlier he had telephoned her and told her that if she would not come back to him, he would throw himself under a train. When she confirmed that she was not coming back, he had done just that, leaving her name and address at his flat as the next of kin.

Another instance was early one morning having decided that in view of the time and that the lady I was going to see was not living at the same address as her husband who had just died, I had no need for a neighbour. I knocked on the door and in due course a head appeared at the upstairs window and asked me what I wanted. I explained it might be better if we could talk a little more in private so with some reluctance she came downstairs and I told her the sad news. There was a great intake of breath and I thought that she was going to faint. Instead, she shouted upstairs, 'Mary, come on down, at last, the old bastard is dead, Yippee!' I gathered that they had had their differences, and having

34

refused a fried breakfast and toast and marmalade, she said, 'I expect you think I'm a little callous.'

I said, 'Good heavens, no.' And rode away with a wry smile!

The smile continued for the rest of the day as a few moments after leaving my grieving widow and family I was called to an accident between two cars. The driver of one had run off. At the scene, sure enough, there was a car with its driver's door open and a very irate second car driver. I had just started to talk to him when a second man appeared, very out of breath, and between gasps he explained that he was the second driver and as the factory where he worked was just down the road, he had run there to 'clock in', as he knew the accident would take some time to sort out and it was better if he was being paid, as the firm fined employees who were late. One of the better excuses!

*   *   *

Each town has at least one area where the locals are noted for their enterprise and able to deal with whatever crisis. A lorry loaded with cartons of Tate and Lyle golden syrup had lost several when the securing rope broke. There were tins all over the road and the driver was about to be reported for having an insecure load. As the police and he looked up the road to see the evidence, every tin, battered, bent and untouched by the fall had all disappeared. Was it by coincidence that the children were coming home from school. All I can say is that for a couple of days if a policeman knocked on a door at teatime there did seem to me a little delay before the door was answered, the sort of time it would take to put back into the larder an item from the tea table perhaps!

There was no prosecution of the lorry driver, for lack of evidence!

At 3.00 a.m. one day I attended a house where an elderly lady had fallen out of bed. Her husband, being frail, was unable to put her back into bed and she was unable to assist. The call came to the police station and with smiles all round she was tucked up back in bed. Some three weeks later the calls during the night were monitored centrally and it was discovered that our dear old lady managed to fall out of bed about once a month and got her husband to ring up different police stations for help, so our turn came once every three months. It fell to me to go and see her. She explained that the truth was that she rather enjoyed being lifted back in bed by two young police officers. We struck a deal that if she put a pillow on the floor the evening she was going to fall out of bed, she perhaps could lie there until having had her husband's call, we would come and help and if there was a delay she could wait in reasonable comfort.

From then on when we saw her, we would have to tell what we had been doing. Many young officers learnt from her that life is not always what it seems. Sadly she died some months after our deal.

Another call in the early hours resulted in my climbing a ladder to a first floor bedroom as the daughter of the house was threatening suicide and would not open her bedroom door for her parents. They told her that they had phoned the police, and upon climbing through the window, I recall she was wearing a very new-looking nightie, her hair and make-up did not seem very consistent with a suicide. With some haste and her indicating that there was no real hurry, I managed to open her bedroom door and let her parents in. Whenever, I pass the house, to this day I still have to smile to myself, and wonder what happened to her over the years.

*   *   *

Radio calls to 'sudden deaths' always sent the heart racing the message often ended with 'ambulance attending'. It was sometimes suggested by the critics of the emergency services that we used to race to the scene to see who could get there last. Not so on this occasion. A doctor was in attendance and we arrived together and were ushered to the garden, where an elderly man was lying face down on the grass near a rose garden. The doctor, who was new to the practice, explained that the man suffered from many problems, not least a weak heart, and as he had been seen by a colleague within the past few days it was possible that he would be able to issue a death certificate which meant that I did not have to worry about coroner's reports, etc.

On reaching our man we turned him over on his back and there was a very large hole in his chest and under the body was a revolver. After we had both recovered from this sight, I regret that I told him that I was glad that he was not my doctor. When he asked why, I explained that if he was unable to tell the difference between a gunshot wound and a heart attack, I wouldn't stand much chance. He forgave me but whenever we met in the months ahead I was reminded by him of his skills as a doctor. Serve me right!

A call to the car one evening sent us to a local pub where an elderly man was at odds with the world having had a little too much to drink. He told us about his army days during the war and the injury he had sustained. We decided to take him home which was about five miles. Two weeks later the call was repeated from the same public house by the same gentleman who said upon our arrival, 'At last my car ride home.' When we declined we became 'Fascist pigs'. I helped rid the world of your type.' We got a taxi for him and on his way he went.

Some six weeks later we were called to his address and sadly our friend had collapsed and died. His wife told us that due to his wounds he had been unable to do anything around the home. In passing she mentioned that he was a great admirer of the police and the job they had to do in these trying days. This did cause us to smile secretly but at the *post-mortem* I had explained to the pathologist about his injury and at the conclusion it was pointed out to me that there was no sign both internally or externally of any war injury. It was not relevant to discuss this with his family. He had died of 'natural causes'.

I often found that the investigation of a suicide or sudden death was much more like a murder investigation only carried out in the first place by yourself, with of course help, but generally you had to request it. There was an elderly man found lying in front of his gas oven, the gas was switched on full and gas was the cause of his death. There was no history of distress, in fact the very opposite. There were no signs of the gaps above and under the doors being blocked off to stop the gas escaping from the room. I tested the gas tap on and off there was no problem and I mentioned my concern to the duty sergeant of the day and together we tried to reconstruct what might have happened. Whilst kneeling on the floor I put my head right into the oven and used a torch to look right down the back on top of gas outlets and there was an uncooked small meat pie and several used matches. Had our poor man just been trying to light the oven to cook himself a meal? That incident always reminded me of was there a life policy that excluded suicide. Families have been known to try to get a suicide look like an accident or a natural death.

A lady with marriage problems had threatened her husband that she would take her own life if he did not stop seeing another woman. This was well-documented and one day she threatened again as he walked out of the door. So he gave her some money to put in the gas meter. This she did and died, leaving a note that he had helped her. This case led to many enquiries and much looking at law books but lacked that extra evidence that was needed for a prosecution. Perhaps there was none to find, but I always wondered.

How do you get a large man who has hanged himself from a branch of a tree some 30 feet from the ground? The text-book says preserve the knot for evidence. The tree concerned is in the middle of a forest and no vehicle can get near. With the help of the fire brigade, ropes, ladders and safety harness our man is in the process of being cut down when the rope holding him breaks and he crashes to the ground, breaking every bone in his body. Who has to tell the pathologist this rather sad story and receive the reply, 'It's a good job, I can tell injuries after death, constable.'

Around 7.00 one morning a girl complains that a man has exposed himself to her from the window of a flat nearby. A knock on the door flat produces a man holding a paint brush, who denies everything.

A very long statement was taken from him and of course the young lady and at last there is a difference between her description of the clothes he wore to those he was wearing when he was challenged. It was in fact his flat mate who had left for work just after the offence and prior to our arrival.

A few evenings later, outside a pub, I had parked J.77 in a hurry to assist restore peace to a good fight and upon my return there it was lying on the ground with minor damage and a broken headlamp. I mentioned this to my superior who was quite sure that I was mistaken. Surely it had been knocked over in the general melee of the incident. I was silly not to have noticed that myself.

Not all court cases end in disaster and I have told this story a number of times to try to help others when all seems lost. The man concerned had been convicted for drunken driving and disqualified for twelve months. This was the end of his world as he was a buyer of land for a building firm and I had stopped him earning his living. In those days application to a court could be made for restoration of the driving licence after half the sentence had been completed. Our man had made such an application and I was required to attend court to remind the magistrates of the circumstances of the case, so that they could decide. Upon my arrival, I was greeted like a lost friend, arm around my shoulders. When I expressed surprise he explained that having lost his licence he had been forced to use train and bus and had seen and purchased so much land in the past six months that he would never have seen from the road that the firm had asked him to become a director!

It was about this time that an incident occurred that I have always felt a little 'guilty' about ever since. There was a owner of a local bookshop who had been a policeman for many years and one day I teased him that with all these 'naughty' magazines about he had failed in his duty to provide for the poor copper on night duty who went round trying all the doors within the town centre, and he could not even put a magazine inside the shop window to help cheer up a very boring night duty.

A few days later, a suitable magazine appeared inside the window of the door. Today, one would not even notice the girl almost not wearing a swimsuit. As the weeks passed the picture was joined by others until the whole of the inside of the glass door was suitably displayed. In my own defence I did wonder if he was not taking things a little far. However, I did not do anything and one day when I went on duty at 3.00 p.m. to my alarm I noticed that in the 'day book' my shop-owner had been arrested for selling or displaying indecent pictures. I expected a formal interview, or worse over the days ahead. Nothing happened and after some weeks my friend appeared in court and was fined

£200, a lot of money then. I wondered about his pension and I was showing every sign of having a conscience. After a suitable delay, and off duty, I went into a certain bookshop to make my peace when I was greeted with a great smile and learnt that the pension was safe as you only lost it if you went to prison. As for the fine, I should be pleased that as a businessman he had made a fortune out of my idea. It seems that after the first window display he had been asked by young men working in a local factory for pictures to put inside their locker doors and a considerable rivalry had developed between the many hundreds of workers and he had a very difficult job keeping up with the demand.

From that day on I had no more bright ideas for shop-keepers or businessmen!

I have already written about 'death messages' but the following is rather hard to believe. It concerns a young man who had committed suicide by fixing the rubber hose from the exhaust pipe inside the car. Early one morning his parents had discovered him inside the garage. There was a note from him indicating that this was the only way out as his girlfriend had given him up as he was too old for her by some five years. As she lived locally I called upon her at her parents' home, and when in front of her mother, I told her the sad news she said, 'That's just the sort of stupid thing he would do.' I remember saying to the body in the mortuary that he wouldn't understand but he was probably better off where he was.

5

Ghosts and Chiefs

There had been a number of articles recently making, I felt, very sarcastic comments about the many ghost stories, mostly untrue. One concerned a motorist who saw a young girl waiting at a bus-stop, late at night. He gave her a lift only to find that she disappeared *en route* and the motorist found out that a girl of that description had been killed at that spot a year ago to the day. I suggest had the author spent many nights outside in the warm and cold he might have had a real incident to pour scorn upon.

I will tell the story as it happened, around 2.00 a.m. I was called to go to a house that was just outside our police district as there was a disturbance. Upon arrival in a very select housing estate, I found a motor cycle combination, its rider in a shouting match with a very distressed man, while upstairs shouting out of the bedroom window was a lady almost beside herself with grief and rage.

The rider of the motor cycle combination had called at their house to try and explain that he had seen a young lady waiting at a bus-stop at Riley on his way home from a late duty shift with the railway. He had three daughters of his own so he had stopped and explained that he did not think that there were any more buses at that time of night. She had accepted his offer of a lift back to her home, had given him the address and off they had set. He talked to her

42

a couple of times about the way and when he turned to speak to her for the third time, she had been sitting on the pillion seat and had gone. He had retraced his journey. Being unable to find her, he had dialled 999 for the police, and then while they and he searched he had decided to call at the address to see if she had arrived home.

He came to the police station to help us with our enquiries when we learnt that the distressed couple had indeed lost a daughter killed by a lorry, at that bus-stop around 2.00 p.m. a year to the day prior to this incident. I was sure that we had a pervert, or other sick man, enjoying the distress he was giving. With others, we checked on him and the incident. Had he read about it, etc? After checking everything we could he went on his way and there was not any evidence to justify prosecution. We even checked where we could on friends and relatives to see whether we could find a connection. I would not be too quick to pour scorn on all ghost stories.

Two incidents come to mind when the law to me can seem unfair and at the same time you could understand the reason but it does not make the lot of a policeman any happier. The first followed a call to a housing estate under construction where two men were at the houses during a weekend and seemed to be pulling out radiators and other fittings and loading them into a van. The two men had a small plumbing business and had put their money into buying radiators and other plumbing items for their contract. They had just discovered the site owners were going bankrupt and they would lose everything and any possible payment by the receiver in the future would be too late for them. They had decided to take out what they could from the houses under construction that they had installed to try and salvage something. They already had lost a month's wages. It seems that at that time as they had not opened the letter from the receiver it would have been difficult to proceed under the criminal law.

The second concerned a young couple who had spent their savings on buying a second-hand car from a dealer. The car had been sold to the dealer by the previous owner whilst still on hire purchase. If the couple had quickly sold on to another they would have got some money and as they had not known of the hire purchase they would have acted in good faith. As it was, the car was reclaimed by the hire purchase company. The dealer would not entertain any claim from the couple and they had no funds to go to law and they learnt a hard lesson very early on. Many years later I came across a car dealer who had written above his car lot. 'My reputation is your guarantee'. When he was caught selling a wreck of a car his defence was, 'My reputation is that I'm a complete crook'. So much for trade descriptions.

There was another incident concerning a coach, in broad daylight, parked on the grass verge beside the main road. The keys were in the ignition but there was no sign of the driver. A radioed vehicle check showed that it was not stolen. I had parked J.77 behind it and was about to get the owner called by phone when suddenly I thought I saw it move slightly. Thinking I was seeing things, I waited and it moved slightly again. I opened the rear doors of the luggage compartment and there, in all their naked glory, were a couple very busy and my opening the doors had caused slight difficulties. From that day on I always had a friendly wave from our local coach driver and a great scowl from a certain lady when I drove past a certain bus stop at 5.30 p.m. outside her place of business. Indeed, this developed into her turning her back towards the road if she saw a police bike coming towards her. I felt that the other people at the bus-stop must find her behaviour rather unusual. I wonder if they asked her why.

Tea time could be a difficult time and I recall being sent

to a 'domestic dispute' when a husband had returned from work and found his wife sitting in front of the television watching her programme instead of getting his dinner ready. He had picked up the television and thrown it straight through the window, which of course was shut at the time. The rather bruised television was sitting in the front garden surrounded by glass and wooden window-frame splinters. He let me know in no uncertain terms that I was not welcome within his home, and anyway, 'Wouldn't you do that if your dinner was not ready?' Having made sure that the lady involved was not hurt, I went on my way.

At that time one had to make sure that you were on the move or well away from the scene of the incident, if not every now again as you began to 'transmit' details of the incident, all the screens of the neighbour's televisions would black out, and they would hear your voice, giving very gossip worthy details.

Another difficulty could be parking a police vehicle outside a house, perhaps just to pass on a message. There was always a neighbour ready to believe that what they had always suspected was now coming true. You could always see the curtains move as you got back to your vehicle. One householder was so worried about this when I told her that I would have to come back that I asked her which neighbour she was worried about. When I returned I parked outside her house and walked to the place of my visit. Upon my return there was a lady standing next to the police vehicle saying in a loud voice to no one in particular, 'He's not with me.'

*   *   *

Even off duty the police life can have or cause one or two difficulties. My wife had asked me to go into the hospital as a visitor and see the husband of a friend of hers who was a little fed up with only female visitors. Having run out of excuses or reasons for not going I duly breezed in to see him to spread the good cheer.

When he saw me he said, 'I know you, you stopped me for speeding.' I thought, 'Oh! no, I'm in for a great visit.' Then I was informed that he had been on his way home and had perhaps just been driving just a little bit over the limit when I had stopped him. I had examined his driving licence and seeing his address, I had said, 'I know you now, you know me, so, I feel sure that there will be no more speeding, locally, will there, sir!' He had confirmed there would be no reason for me to stop him in the future. We had parted on good terms and he told me that I had been a real problem to him, in that had I booked him he would have a good moan, but instead every time he came within a mile or so of home he would slow down just in case I was waiting for him. I must say that I felt my action was on the pompous side. He, however, felt that it was good local policing. We did remain friends thereafter.

A rather similar type of incident can give rise to all sorts of emotion and justice seems unfair crooked or even stupid and possibly correct depending on your point of view. A motorist passing through the town centre late at night felt that as he went by an electrical shop he was sure that he had seen a hand emerge from the darkness behind the window display and remove a radio. Upon his arrival home he telephoned the police and as a result a gang of thieves were caught and a number of other crimes were also cleared up. The following morning our motorist was caught in a radar trap and due to his motoring record he was, if convicted, going to be disqualified. Hard luck say some. Others say for goodness sake what about public relations? Others cannot see that there is any connection. He was prosecuted. Two branches of the police force could not agree!

There were a number of instances when I had hoped that my superiors might have supported me a little more and had even hoped that the complaint might be denied rather than smoothed over. I regret those days do not seem to be with us now and possibly even further away than they were then.

I am not of course without an axe to grind but when I joined the police I was sworn in as a 'constable' at the Guildhall at Guildford, in front of those who matter, that I would 'Protect life and property'.

I had attended a road traffic accident at around 9.00 one morning. A boy aged about eight years had been injured and taken to hospital with quite serious leg injuries. There was nobody at home. Neighbours had told me that his parents caught a train to London and they did not know of other relatives or friends. I contacted the school and they only had his home address as their point of contact. I had decided to visit the boy in hospital and try and find how I could find one or both his parents. When I got there he was in great pain and the hospital wanted a 'consent' form completed for an operation. I signed the form on behalf of the parents and, having spoken with the lad, I eventually got in contact with his mother at work.

All had gone well, or so I thought until the next day I was told that there had been a complaint against me for misuse of authority. The parents had religious objections to surgery etc. In their view, as their son was not in a life-threatening situation, I should have waited.

The next day I was at a meeting with the parents and my superiors when I was told off, I agree rather mildly. They went away happy and I've had a chip on my shoulder ever since. I could see that the action of my superiors had stopped an official complaint and even that my record would have been marked over the incident but it would have been greatly appreciated if my action could have been endorsed as the right thing to do. I was not aware that my duties included being able to make medical judgements of that kind.

Around 4.00 one morning, just over our boundary with the Metropolitan police, with a colleague we spied one of their Vellocette motor cycles parked beside the kerb, outside a bus-shelter. Upon closer examination we found, stretched out on the seat inside the shelter a police officer, fast asleep. I must confess that I gently rolled his motorcycle, keeping the engine switched off, down the hill and hid it in a side road. I then returned to the scene with due noise and a certain police officer woke up with a start and after a few minutes, realized his bike had gone. His panic was such that he could picture his dismissal and my colleague did not help by suggesting that perhaps the culprit was at that moment speeding towards the heart of the Metropolitan Police. For a few minutes, which we knew were hours to him, we helped him search up and down the road for it. I 'discovered' it and called him down to the scene. His thanks and our promise of keeping quiet were such that by the time we left I think he had started to wonder if there was not more to the incident that he had first thought.

At this point it is only fair to relate a police story that is passed down the generations. It concerns the river Thames, when on the north bank it is within the Metropolitan Police area and to the south, the Surrey Constabulary. A body drifting down the river belongs to neither until it touches the north or south bank. It seems that a poor soul had drowned and in such cases it is known almost to the hour when the body will surface. After a day or so, the location of its appearance can be estimated with reasonable accuracy.

Early one morning following such an incident an officer from Surrey is detailed to keep watch on the river and after an hour or so he sees the body bobbing down the middle of the river and it is alleged at this point that he threw a stone or two just to get it to drift to the north shore when a call could be made to the other force saying they had a visitor on their shore. Things were going well when suddenly, a police helmet appeared from behind a bush on the north bank and a voice shouted, 'Leave the bloody thing alone. It's taken me all night to get it back in the middle!' The result of the contest is not known.

During a night duty it was the custom to call upon others who also worked at night. A cup of tea and friendly chat never went amiss. The visits could be to bakers, security officer, railway workers, night watchmen, etc. In a factory that made plastic objects from garden gnomes to flower pots there was one night worker there to feed the machines. We used to see him around 3.00 a.m. have a chat and he seemed pleased to have someone to talk to. One morning upon arrival, the whole workshop was full of flower pots, about five feet high. The machine was still spitting them out by the hundreds, or so it appeared. Sadly our man had died from natural causes and was hidden from view lying on the floor under all those pots. It seemed an age before the machine could be switched off.

One very wet evening the house of a very important local dignitary had been broken into, the sort of person whom you have never heard of until then. Anyway, everyone was running around being busy when I was called to go to the house and on going up the drive I ran over a black fur-coated animal. All I needed was to arrive having just run over their beloved cat. I stopped and found with some relief that it was a fur stole, wet and bedraggled but at least it was not the cat. Upon my arrival at the mansion the lady gave a scream of delight. I had it seems found her prize mink stole. I managed to brush off the tread of the tyre before handing it over to a 'Well done, constable.'

A very boring part of being a policeman is pounding the beat and senior officers would always refer to one as the 'Backbone of the force'. Yet if any traffic or CID officer was in disgrace he was always returned to patrol duties.

However, not many years before I joined the Surrey Constabulary they had taken over the borough police of Guildford that had looked after the town and other towns, including Reigate. The officers taken over always seemed to look at us as if we had upset their lives, which of course the amalgamation had. Anyway I always remember with a smile and admiration an elderly constable who patrolled Guildford High Street. Not both sides or even the whole length, his patrol was some 300 yards on the same side of the street everyday. One cold winter's day, I stopped to talk briefly to him, and mentioned that I could not understand how he did not go out of his mind with boredom. He smiled and told me to stand beside him, where he had his back to a wall. This I did and discovered that he was standing in front of a hot air extractor from a shop. He then told me to lift my gaze upwards to the second floor of the shop on the opposite side of the road. This I did. Then he told me to look at the fourth window to the left and there, to my surprise, I could see a lady trying on a brassiere. He smiled, told me that he was warm and had a reasonable view. Now, who was the fool, riding a motor cycle that talked to itself and gave out lots of work?

I had to admit he had a point and can understand that he did not want to be absorbed into a county police force. I also understood that in his young days you had to wait your turn to be allowed to patrol the High Street.

*   *   *

Hot summer nights could bring their share of a little fun in that the area had a fair number of lakes and rivers and the heat of night would tempt the young to do a spot of nude bathing, which was fine until they would choose a privately-owned lake and without exception there would be a complaint in the early hours of the morning. Upon arrival all the bathers would of course disappear into the night and the bushes, which added to the fun and risk. A good number of them had borrowed their 'wheels' from their parents or family. They would not emerge from the bushes even when asked politely. There was no point in trying to find them yourself, so you would make a note of the registration number of a car, and then in a loud voice you would pretend you were using the radio and ask, 'Vehicle check please, request you to contact the registered owner.' You would then shout out the registration number and within a few minutes a rather sheepish couple would emerge from the bushes and explain that the car was not theirs and Mummy and Daddy, might not understand. The remaining couples would then emerge and we would make a great thing of taking their names and addresses and rarely did anything further. I have wondered if their parents ever wondered why they were so co-operative for a few days after they had borrowed the car.

*   *   *

The human being can be a strange animal when it feels under threat or pressure. I had stopped a motorist for exceeding the speed limit and if he had a valid insurance, etc., a warning would have probably met the situation. As I walked up to him, he started.

'Why haven't you got better things to do than harass poor motorists? What about all the murderers running around? At this point the calm, cool, very polite manner takes over and in due course I asked to see inside the boot of his car, hinting perhaps that a felon could be hiding

51

there, unknown to him of course. Upon opening the boot there was six brand new car batteries, still with wrapping on. He explained that the car was very light on the back end and that he used to carry them as ballast in case it was wet. Back at the police station when it had been confirmed that he had stolen them from a garage where he worked, I told him that had he been only reasonably polite I doubted that I would have asked to see in the boot. He told me that he could not help it. It was the officious way that I had put the police bike on its stand.

A call had sent me to the railway station when a child had been reported seen walking along the railway line. I was assured that the electricity had been switched off, so off I walked in the centre of the track and after about 20 minutes there was no sign of any child. A few minutes later, rather as one sees in western films, I heard or rather felt a vibration from the stones beneath the rails. Upon turning round there, travelling slowly towards me, was the 10.50 a.m. to Waterloo. I stepped with due haste off the track, the train stopped beside me and the driver leaned out of the cab and offered me a lift. I had never realized how high a train is off the ground until that moment. I then realized that of course the current had been switched back on, and thought what I might have done. I aired my fears to the driver who explained that they took great pride in the time schedule and one shocked copper was not an unreasonable price to pay. In revenge I managed to get him to let me drive the train a little way and so achieved a boyhood ambition and also made my Father 'green' with envy at beating him to this important landmark of life.

Father used to avoid travelling within my area if he could. He never admitted it but I think he was worried for being prosecuted for both my and his reputation. One day however, I saw his car parked, so wrote out a ticket and placed it under the windscreen wiper. On his return, with two friends, he was so annoyed that I might find out about it that he stuffed it in his pocket and carried on. His friends had not noticed. That night, on emptying his pockets, he came across the ticket and I can only guess what he said to himself, when he read, 'Did unlawfully use on a public road, a dirty car, contrary to Section 1, of Bucket & Sponge Act, 1066.

One summer morning, travelling from Guildford to Leatherhead on the A246, in front of me was a familiar car towing a boat. I was sure that it belonged to the chief constable, only the number plate on the rear of the trailer did not match with that of the car. What should I do? Was it a test to see whether I would have the bottle to stop him and do something or should I take the next turning left and pretend I had seen nothing? With some fear and trepidation I decided to overtake and signalled the driver to stop. I pulled up J.77 onto its stand and walked back to the driver, and there was no mistaking the driver.

I saluted and said, 'Good morning sir, I believe the number-plate on the trailer is incorrect to the number of your car.'

He replied, 'Rubbish, you do know who, I am, do you really think I would venture on to the road if everything was not A1?' I remember saying that did he think I would stop the chief constable if I were not sure? He took the point and together we examined the scene of the crime and found that I was correct. I told him that the facts would be reported, saluted and rode away with all speed, only to be called via the radio within minutes to report to the superintendent.

This I did and his opening remark was, 'You believe in living dangerously?' I explained my predicament. He understood and I had to write the report there and then. A few weeks later I was advised that a caution would suffice in this case and my inspector told me that there had been a note from the chief, saying, 'Compliment the officer on his keen observation'.

6

Supermarket and Sheriffs

There was another incident which resulted in the chief constable writing about me.

The day before I started two weeks' leave, when the family were all packed to go away, I was on early shift 7.00 a.m. to 3.00 p.m. At around 2.00 p.m. I was hiding on Headley Heath enjoying the sunshine when every mobile unit within our area was called for 'location'. I was relieved to hear other units being on the main roads and town centres, so it is easy to imagine my dismay when with no hesitation they told me that there was a man in the car, nearby, a possible suicide. I arrived within a few minutes and there was the car with the hose from the exhaust and the driver slumped over the wheel. I remember thinking death, inquest, no leave, broke open the door and pulled the man out, switched off the engine, rather roughly put him on the ground and started resuscitation, cursing to myself about my leave. He suddenly moved. I worked really hard. An ambulance was called and off to hospital he went. Much relieved, I completed my report and off on holiday I went. Upon my return the sergeant advised me that the chief had written a few words on the report and in large green ink was written, 'Well done, a life saved'. The sergeant asked me if that had given me a good feeling.

I mumbled something and he said, 'Good, you will want

to know that your man got out of hospital and threw himself under a train and died.' That good feeling disappeared instantly.

My way of dealing with death in all its forms was humour – sick maybe, but it was my way of being able to cope. At this time if you were called or detailed to a death, you were the coroner's officer, dealt with the relatives, the inquest and all the emotions surrounding tragedy.

One of the first suicides I was called to was an elderly lady who had decided to end it all by use of the gas oven. Upon my arrival I broke in and smelling the gas, threw my truncheon through the glass of the back window. After all necessary work had been done at the scene the sergeant asked me if I had found the truncheon. I confirmed that I had not so he advised me to look and in future never ever let go of it. On looking into the garden it was so overgrown that the next day in my own time it took me some two hours to find it. The police always had a way of keeping the individual on a level that made sense.

Not long after this incident another occurred when a lady with her cats had done the same thing, only the meter had run out just after her death, but her cats had survived. Air had come through the top of a door. Several days had gone by prior to us being called and the cats in their hunger had started to attack her body for food. Before getting into the house they had to be caught. I do not need to explain the details.

I had again forgotten all about horses so, yet again, I went cold when the radio sent me to a runaway horse complete with young rider still on board. They were careering down a main road causing just a little chaos and my horror can be imagined when on joining the road concerned, there in front of me, was a pony in full flight with a rider clinging round its neck. I got alongside them and with great stupidity I took my hand off the handlebars of J.77 and took hold of the reins that were trailing. Slowly, the horse stopped. It really was one of the most silly things to do. The pony, could at any moment have pulled me off the bike, or run in front, and yet it worked. The gods must have been looking after me, and perhaps I had also exorcized my, or rather the horse's ghost for Constable 697!

One summer evening I attended a local supermarket, when some four young people aged about nine years had been caught, shoplifting a bag of crisps and a drink. I had a car and after the usual enquiries the young people got into the car and I drove them to the police station. I left them sitting inside the car with a colleague keeping an eye on them and went into the station to find a mentor of mine and told him that I had a surprise for him. He told me that with all his years in the police force nothing would surprise him but when I explained that I thought I might, as I had his son and friends in the car outside, the speed from which he came round his desk and to the front door gave me the impression that I had indeed surprised him.

I always liked the postscript to this incident. The father took his son back to the supermarket a few days later and managed to get the manager to agree that he could speak to all the staff for a minute.

The father explained to the young ladies on the checkouts that if they ever saw this young man, standing beside him, in their store again they had his permission to take his trousers down and give him a hiding. The reaction of the staff was of genuine amusement. As for the son, it was rumoured that even after twenty years he still cannot go into a store that carries a particular name over the door. I do wonder what sort of comment would be made today if similar action was taken. It did work, rather too well.

I had attended a particular nasty accident involving a number of cars and there had been many injuries, some very serious, and a radio call directed me to a garage graveyard where a number of cars had been taken. My task was to sort through the front of one car in particular to look for a set of false teeth so that surgeons could start, rebuilding a driver's mouth and face. This very unpleasant task, sorting out glass, pieces of humans, metal, wood and everything else is part of one's duty. They do not mention that sort of task when you join! So every now and again just think before you react to being asked to make a cup of tea. Your unwritten job description could be worse!

Riding uphill towards the High Street one morning, flying towards me, getting lower and lower and the closing speed was much too fast for my skills, was a swan in full flight. It might look magnificent as a rule but coming straight for you is another thing. We met and both fell down on to the ground. He got up first, looked at me and J.77 with disdain and his look was such that I was at least guilty of dangerous driving. My problem was that if I did not get a witness, if not to the accident at least to the swan strutting around, otherwise I would never be believed, my superiors would have a field-day with my report. My evidence having recovered, was, I'm sure about to fly off, so with a piece of chocolate I delayed him enough for the investigating officer at least to see him. He did not press any charges but I was far from popular, not only for the damage to the motorcycle but also that I was not believed and had to endure remarks for several weeks as to had I hit any tigers, elephants or possibly a budgie, and the end of duty.

*   *   *

I was always very impressed with the knowledge and common sense of prisoners one came across. They were very well-informed on the benefits of society and charities and also the good and bad points of particular prisons. For example, in early December, you find 'gentlemen of the road' making their way towards Norwich. They would break a shop window locally, for bed and breakfast needs, but Norwich was their aim around the 23rd or 24th December, not for the character of the prison staff but because it served by far the best Christmas dinner.

On the charge sheet, there was a space for 'Religion' and you would expect C of E or R C to be advised but no, they would often make you write down a branch or section that you had never heard of. When you queried this you were soon informed that their nomination was the best payer by way of cash donation to a member of their faith when discharged from prison.

Due to lack of candidates, I was for a few days made an 'Acting sergeant' and I duly reported for one night duty, and around 3.00 a.m. there was a frantic 999 call. A man was trying to break into a house and the duty inspector decided with a constable to attend, leaving me in charge of the police station. In due course they returned with a man more than a little drunk. I was told to put him in the cells, make out a charge sheet, filling in his particulars when he was sober. The inspector would get him in front of the court at 10.00 the following morning. The public had to be protected from villains such as he, frightening householders at night. The inspector went off duty and I started to fill in the charge sheet and around 4.00 a.m. my prisoner was a little better at answering my questions and I started to become very uneasy. At 7.00 a.m. I released him and had him taken home by police car. Shortly afterwards the inspector contacted me about progress. He presumed all had gone well and when I started to explain he exploded at my action and it took several minutes for me to calm him down and explain that our friend was in fact the husband of the complainant, lived with her at the same address. As he was coming home 'worse for wear' from an unauthorized night out with the boys, so she had decided to teach him a lesson, by pretending she didn't know him and he was too drunk to know! I just escaped, with others, from playing a leading part in a good story for the media.

We do of course never stop learning and one day in the company of a long serving colleague we stopped a car, whereupon the driver lent across the passengers' seat and tore off the tax disc and popped it into his mouth. My quick thinking companion got to him quickly, slapped him on the back, in a very similar manner as when meeting an old friend. The paper pellet was then recovered. In due course the pellet dried out on the radiator at the police station. He had stolen the disc from his works.

One evening on the main A24 road a car pulled out of a line and started to overtake all the other traffic. When you are on or in a police vehicle as you start to follow a possible felon on wheels all the drivers you overtake you can see by their faces and the way they pull over to let you pass that they are all great supporters in your dispensing of justice to the other fellow. I duly overtook the line of cars and stopped the car concerned. As all the overtaken cars passed you could feel that 'Serve you right' as they glanced to their left and put their feet down.

As I walked back towards the driver, he started to get out of the car and said, 'Officer, my wife is pregnant.' I looked across at her and, yes, she was pregnant but her serene look and charming smile which included a large wink, seemed to be giving me the message, 'Yes it is true, but not yet.'

I asked the driver if he wanted me to escort him to the hospital. I could use the siren, blue light and ask for assistance, if need be.

He looked at me and said, 'Can you spare the time?' I assured him that I could, whereupon he said, 'Sod it, just my luck to find a knight riding a bloody bike.' He confessed that the emergency was not anticipated for another month, and his lady passenger just kept smiling as I decided that he merited a lecture on road safety and child care.

There is an unwritten rule that there should be no arrests, other than for serious crime, that means keeping a person in custody over the Christmas period, or even for Christmas Day.

Christmas Eve has always been a good night for a little celebration and one of our local friends was no exception other than around midnight he was standing at the traffic lights, shouting at motorists as they stopped for a red light, 'Can't find a colour you like, mate.' After a few minutes his display included climbing up the traffic light to give it a clean, thus saving the council a few pounds! He was arrested, or rather put into the back of a police car, when after a few minutes he fell into a deep sleep. My intention was to get him home as soon as possible. Things did not go my way, there was a lost child, found within a few minutes, a lady locked out of her house, a minor road accident and so on. Each incident was dealt with the usual efficiency and not a soul seemed to notice this rather smelly man, sitting in the back of the police car, snoring his head off. If they did, they were too polite to say anything.

It was around 2.00 a.m. that there was a gap in incidents to take him home. I had a real struggle to get him out of the rear of the car and in all the pulling out his foot got caught behind the driver's seat, but one more heavy heave sorted him out and I struggled up to his front door, and his wife, pleased to see him, wished me a 'Merry Christmas.'

The rest of the night went without too many problems – a noisy party or two and around 6.00 a.m. a vicar who jumped some traffic lights that were on red. He was not very concerned that he had broken the law, or that he may have caused an accident.

'As I was on the Lord's work, there would be a very

important person looking after my welfare, with a lot more influence than you would ever have.' I was not prepared to argue and he went on his way to meet his flock.

Some two weeks later a familiar figure was seen limping down the High Street. We met and he told me that his wife had told him that I had taken him home a little worse for wear but ever since his foot had hurt and the doctor had told him that he had a severe strain. Did I have any idea as to how he might have hurt his foot? To my shame, I shook my head and told him about the traffic lights. He was happy that he himself must have sustained his injury then.

*　　*　　*

I very much hope that in my normal state I am not a bully. There was, however, one occasion when I have to admit to bullying one of Her Majesty's civil servants.

A fatal accident had happened when the rider of a motor cycle was killed. He was aged about 30 and had elderly parents who depended on him for financial support. Their pensions did not pay much more than the rent. Their son was of course 'the apple of their eye' and his death had hit them hard. I was making the arrangements for an inquest and went to see them, when they related that they were unable to get any assistance from the system. As there had been no inquest, or proof of death, there would be no help yet.

I went to see the 'system' who was an offensive, sarcastic young man who took obvious pleasure in explaining to a 'thick copper' that there was not even a report in the local paper yet, which if he used his influence, might be able to get his superiors to accept and give some assistance to the parents. I asked if my word could be accepted in the same way, as that of a young reporter on the local paper.

He replied, 'Hardly, you are only a Constable!'

I freely admit that at this point I went round behind his desk and forced him into a police car which conveyed him to the mortuary where a little reluctantly he went very pale as I pulled open the drawer of the 'freezer' and made him look at the label tied to the body. It was of course unfortunate that at that time there were a number of other residents who were not a pretty sight. My friend agreed that perhaps under the circumstances a little assistance might be available for the victim's next of kin. I took him back to his office to ensure that he kept his word. Upon leaving him I guessed that I just might be the subject of a complaint within a day or so. An hour would have been more accurate. I was rightly reprimanded and warned about my future conduct! I felt that, on balance, it was worth it.

A foggy November night I was sent to an accident where a number of cars and a lorry were involved. The driver of the lorry was impaled on his steering wheel. The accident was on a narrow road and the weather conditions were such that at anytime I expected further vehicles to join the misfortune. However, there was an elderly gentleman in the back of a large black car moaning about his leg hurting when he had been thrown forward in the accident. I pointed out that he would be dealt with as soon as possible and if he had the injuries sustained by the lorry driver he would have a bigger problem. He fell quiet and not long afterwards the situation improved. Assistance arrived at the same time as the ambulance took the injured to hospital. A start was made on the paperwork and later that evening I learnt that the passenger in the car was a high sheriff and the driver was of course his chauffeur. In due course a case came to court and as the high sheriff was a principle witness a number of my senior officers had reason to be at court that day, including an assistant chief constable who asked if all had gone well at the scene of the accident.

My important witness gave me a long hard look and replied, 'The constable had a lot on his plate at the time and was not suffering fools gladly.'

The Assistant Chief Constable asked me afterwards, 'What on earth did he mean?'

I assured him that I had no idea. I did appreciate his tact and learnt a little more about life!

*   *   *

There were a number of incidents that gave a view of life that is not always considered or appreciated. There was the suicide of a brilliant young lady who had passed every examination and test from school and university and then failed on one paper for a doctorate. The distress and grief she gave herself and those that loved her makes me ask if failure is an important part of life?

How do you help or advise a family when their crawling young baby puts into its mouth the flex of a standard lamp that has been joined by insulation tape rather than replaced, and gets electrocuted?

Do you tell the parents of a young man, with a drug problem, who has ended his life, leaving a note which tells them in no uncertain terms what he thinks of them, using all the foul mouthed terms imaginable? I suggest no. Of course, you give the note with the records but no good purpose would be served in telling the world at the inquest. Certain papers might appreciate it.

The husband and wife who had gone on holiday reported the house empty to the police, with their friends who lived on the opposite side of the road keeping an eye on the place for them. Around 2.00 a.m. twelve days later the police were called by the husband who had to get up to answer a call of nature and had seen a torch light in the sitting-room in the house opposite. Their friends were not due back for another two days. Cars, and dog-handlers all attended the scene. One man was hiding in the larder, the other behind the couch in the front room. They were both taken away and I went upstairs to have a look round and there, in bed fast asleep, were the owners who had come home early. They had not heard a thing.

An up-and-coming officer confided to me one day that he had never had to serve summons and was there any custom and practice for him to adopt to keep the world at peace? He realized there could be difficulties. I went with him to the house concerned, and reminded him that, having knocked on the door, it was a good idea to take some four quick paces back. He went up to the front door, knocked and stood there, I shouted to him, he took three paces backwards, and at that moment the upstairs landing window opened and a bucket of water splashed onto the concrete in front of him.

Are there any other jobs, that include standing on a railway bridge at 4.00 a.m. as a Royal Train passes underneath, spewing black smoke?

The man cutting his hedge, dressed in shorts one sunny weekend, collapsed and died. Upon his arrival at hospital over £500 in cash was in his back pocket.

The cash was taken to the widow who says, 'Yes, I know, he always carries a good sum. He is an antique dealer.'

She threw the money into the kitchen drawer on top of a larger sum, also in cash.

How do you explain that your very ordinary, nice, friendly public, when involved on picket duty at their place of work, with some dispute with the management, have to be prevented from turning over invalid carriages with the occupants inside?

The local magistrate who lived on the main road where there was a 30 m.p.h. speed limit lived at a house called

Twin Oaks and when a police officer related that he had followed a speeding car from a house called Twin Oaks at a speed in excess of 40 m.p.h., the member of the bench would almost burst with rage and shout, 'Most dangerous stretch of road in the county.'

So much for justice being seen to be done.

Imagine breaking into a house when the occupant is believed to have committed suicide, and on entering you find that had you not climbed through the window you would have received the blast of a shotgun when you opened the door, as the deceased had thought it a good idea if he could take someone with him by attaching a string from the trigger to the door, the gun having been secured with rope and pieces of wood.

You are called to a house, without light, heat and every other floorboard missing, due to being burnt on the fire for warmth and light. The children are carrying all their prized belongings in their pockets otherwise they would be seized and sold by other members of the family.

The next call is to the lord of the manor he thought he heard gunshots. Obviously poachers were in the woods. You went from the humble home to one where your boots were lost in the pile of the carpet.

There were, of course, murders, rapes, incest, house-breaking, indecent assaults and many other incidents that have given me cause to reflect but the time had come to move on. So with considerable misgivings I resigned and some said the real reason was that it had been decided that the call-sign J.77 would be replaced by Delta 22 and that I would never be able to cope with the change.